Predators 101

3 Seconds to Safety

By William J. Riley

Published by Trikke.MI

Copyright

Contents

Introduction

The purpose of this book is to give the average person the confidence to listen to the small voice inside (often called intuition) when it gives safety advice. As a culture, we are reluctant to give credence to intuition because we are science based and the science described herein is still in development. I do not call this method intuition but rather the automatic correlation of all five senses into a single feeling of dread, fear or unease. The degree expressed depends upon the intensity of the input. I will explain some of the science involved which includes the sweat gland system and our sense of what is normal.

Profiling has gotten a bad name because of the illegal use of Race, Religion or Ethnic Origins to decide who should receive extra attention from Law Enforcement. There are two legal and highly valuable types of Profiling that have revolutionized the field of Law Enforcement. They are Geographic Profiling and Behavioral Profiling.

Geographic Profiling uses software developed by Environmental Systems Research Institute (ESRI). The software supports many governmental services from refuse collection to the Fire Department and now is used by many Police Departments. Unless the software is already in use by the jurisdiction it has seen limited use in Law Enforcement because the tools and training required to practice it are expensive. With continued research and acceptance Geographic Profiling will see enormous growth.

Behavioral Profiling is largely hidden from public sight but it is in use by Federal Law Enforcement such as the TSA, the FBI and Intelligence Agencies. As practiced by those agencies, Behavioral Profiling can be a complex science requiring many hours of technical training. The most important factor is that no tools are typically required. No scanners, no communication intercepts, just simple observation of the behavior of individuals. The lack of equipment means that the only barrier to use by ordinary citizens is the training part. The author has developed this book to enable ordinary people (preferably five years of age or older) to understand and use the same principles with some exclusions.

The actual difference between professional use of these techniques and the lay use is the outcome of their use. Law Enforcement uses these techniques to subject suspects to greater examination, sometimes to prevent problems but often to gather enough data to prepare search warrants and to enable them to detain suspects.

The ordinary citizen is not going to question suspects, detain them or hopefully even get close to them. I advise using these techniques to spot potential predators so you can avoid them at all costs. Avoidance of a potential problem is safe, cheap and does no harm.

The Behavior Profiling taught in this book is for ordinary citizens so we will identify criminals to enable escape, not confrontation. Police are charged with investigating and intervening. For citizens, any interaction with criminals is dangerous, potentially expensive and very unpredictable. Television is filled with reports of people taking on criminals when they had the option to call for Police assistance and things went badly. They wind up in court and are often charged with serious crimes. Juries are unpredictable and once charged, you would need a lawyer and you would be tied up in the legal process.

The principles taught here are usable by children and adults. Recent discoveries indicate that six month old babies can detect criminal behavior. Watch for negative reactions expressed by your children, by your family and your friends. Negative reactions may have a simple explanation that does not involve predatory behavior but remember that it is always a possibility. It is safer to move away from possible danger than to escape from it.

Background

General Criminal Behavior

Without going into legal definitions, criminals are people who do not follow society norms. They largely ignore the rules that have been put in place to make human interaction safe and effective. Some people violate laws that they do not value or consider appropriate. They do not consider themselves to be criminals but they open themselves up to police action. I believe the most important benefit from enforcement of all laws is that big criminals commit small crimes. Going through a stop sign gives a legal reason to stop the vehicle. About one third of such stops finds a much bigger crime or criminal.

Predatory Behavior

Criminals often follow a pattern which will allow us to interrupt their behavior before it becomes a personal challenge. It consists of the following stages:

Target Selection – Criminals tend to specialize. Some types of crime require special talents or special training. We will be considering for the most part, those criminals who prey on adults or children with occasional notes on recognizing other types.

Plan – The criminals we are looking for do not usually commit crimes of opportunity. They usually have territories where they are most comfortable and they often display a pattern of time, targets and other factors which assemble into a modus operendi. The planning process usually includes surveillance behavior which is what we are going to look for. This is the best time to interrupt the crime.

Assemble tool box – criminal tools range from escape transportation to weapons and disguises and other elements. There are tools specific to criminal use such as lock picking tools. Unless you are a Locksmith, it is illegal to carry those tools. Similarly, someone carrying bolt cutters is a suspect since there is no common use for them in public.

Deploy – once their plan is ready to execute they proceed to their operating range. This is a difficult phase to interrupt since they are prepared for action and have the will to do whatever it takes to execute their plan.

Act – when criminals get to this stage it is dangerous and difficult to stop. It often takes only seconds and since the criminal chooses the timing, even weapons and training in Martial Arts is often not enough to escape the crime.

Escape – at this stage, reporting to 911 and gathering evidence is usually the only option.

Exploit – once the criminal has escaped they use their gains and prepare to start the cycle over again. One benefit accruing to Law Enforcement is that if two crimes can be connected the chance of finding the perpetrator becomes much greater. The criminal who commits only one crime has the best chance of not being discovered.

If we can interrupt this system during the Target Selection or Plan phases we have the best chance for safety. Target Selection is normally done through surveillance. If we look for all the signs that someone is looking for a target then chances are we will not have to go to defensive procedures. The criminal performs a risk reward analysis once a target is detected and we want to present a high risk low reward profile.

High risk targets are those which are ready, willing and able to defend against predators. Low reward targets are those which do not offer money, jewelry, or whatever the predatory is looking for. Two or more people are higher risk than a single person. The appearance of strength in the person is a deterrent. A relatively weak appearance can be strengthened by having tools such as canes (think big stick).

Criminal Environments

The Broken Window Theory posits that letting an area go to seed and decay, allowing graffiti, broken windows and unkempt grounds, shows that nobody cares about that area and therefore criminals will not be hassled. Evidence shows that maintaining areas properly usually reduces crime and letting them go often increases crime. For the purposes of this discussion, you should avoid areas that are obviously poorly looked after.

Predators typically have preferred hunting areas where they know the territory including escape routes, and areas where prey can be found. Predators can be anywhere but you probably don't have to worry about them inside your home, at the office or at friendly and family gatherings. They like to hunt where the lighting is poor (reduces chances of being identified), close to expressways (good escape routes) and where there is little traffic, few police patrols and little chance of being interrupted. Pickpockets like to work in crowds and embezzlers work in offices but I am not including them in this book as Predators because their behavior is difficult to interpret without special training. I do recommend keeping all strangers at a distance and if you have embezzlement opportunities, keep a close check on all transactions.

Old Criminalistics

There are two methods of fighting crime, preventive and corrective. An old method of preventive crime fighting is called Pin Mapping. Crimes are marked on a map by pins that are color coded for type of crime. Looking at the map one sees problem areas and can begin to look for patterns that allow additional resources to act in a preventive manner. For corrective crime fighting, a detective can use Pin Maps to focus their efforts.

The old preventive side was the Cop on the Beat who knew the troublemakers and their habits well enough to intervene before real trouble broke out and if it did get hot, he knew where to find the guilty parties.

New Criminalistics

The Cop on the Beat has become a rarity but the concept called Community Oriented Policing or COPs is gaining ground. It is an attempt to get some of the preventive benefits by increasing exposure to and interaction with the citizenry. If Police are strangers to the residents there will be little chance to develop trust and gain significant information when crime does occur.

The standard practice today in most communities is for Police to be in squad cars on patrol and act in response to Dispatch when crimes are discovered. This is a reactive centered process and focuses on speedy discovery and reporting of crimes instead of prevention.

The Pin Map has been up graded to true Geographic Profiling. Research into criminal behavior has resulted in a tool called "Path to Crime" which involves tracking and predicting how criminals work in a geographic sense. That concept and using software to track more data and do forecasting has been developed by ESRI.

Geographic Profiling

This is the replacement for Pin Mapping. If a whole bunch of let's say Red Pins (indicating Arson perhaps) showed up in a particular area you could set patrols to watch for potential threats and alert the Fire Department to keep close. These types of maps are still in use for some things but the major limitation is that they can only show location and broadly indicate the crime in question. With the advent of computer mapping, we now can look at much more detail and very specific crime information. The Detective is looking for patterns in the data and if two or more crimes can be connected the chances of finding the perpetrator multiply. Honing analysis tools has been very successful when combined with data on criminal behavior. At a minimum it allows Departments to focus their resources to better effect. One of the most important changes from Pin Mapping to Geographic Profiling was the input of time into the data. As an example, if Police wanted to look for drunk drivers they should look in bar areas between 2 AM and 2:30. If cars were being stolen between 3 and 3:30 it would be well to check the nearest high school.

Behavior Profiling

The newest method of detecting criminal activity is Behavior Profiling and intensive training in this discipline has been presented to Transportation Security Agency agents, FBI, Customs and Border Patrol agents, other agencies both foreign and domestic and some civilian groups such as Mall security. Behavior Profiling is based on extensive studies of human behavior dating back to the late 1940s. Most

Law Enforcement is thinly stretched so it is used to determine which people merit additional investigation.

This book focuses on Behavior Profiling because it can be done with no tools and uses techniques that most people have. Many Local, State and Federal Law Enforcement agencies use Behavior Profiling to some degree or another. Advanced techniques are available but take longer to learn and for the average person, have limited application. Most people do not interact with criminals often enough to develop the skills for micro-analysis such as those shown in television programs. You should not be close enough to criminals to notice small facial expressions nor are you likely to have the tools needed to do voice analysis.

Everyone does behavioral profiling but they refer to it as "a sixth sense". The sixth sense is the total of all five senses that we use in looking at the world. We have been doing that since we were babies. We assign Good, Bad and Neutral to all interactions with people and animals. This book will help you understand the science behind those intuitions that help keep us safe.

Police that are trained in and use Behavioral Profiling use it to identify individuals or groups that need additional attention. Behavioral Criminal Profiling for civilians is focused on avoiding crime by recognizing the potential for criminal behavior and encouraging people to leave the scene before trouble starts.

Police are tasked with interfering to prevent crime but must have suspicions that can be clearly stated or have probable cause before they can question suspects. Civilians do not have Constitutional authority to question other citizens regardless of their suspicions, they are advised to remove themselves from the area and notify authorities of their suspicions.

To that end, we will help you to identify suspicious behavior and help you to communicate your suspicions to the proper authorities so they can take action.

Suspicious behavior is abnormal behavior so we will compare normal behavior with abnormal behavior. The degree of suspicion will relate to the deviation from normal.

Some behavioral profiling procedures are micro level referring to facial signs, and small movements of arms, hands and legs. There is significant benefit in looking into those areas but we focus on detecting criminals at a distance so only rarely will we look at those items. We want you to stay beyond the range where those observations can be made.

The old adage is that to catch a thief you need to think like a thief. That is the specialty of Detectives but if you understand the Behavior Profiling process you will be well trained in detecting suspicious behavior and dangerous areas.

If you had a bodyguard and trouble broke out they would shove you out of harm's way. Don't you think you should do the same thing? Avoid being involved in any criminal interaction.

Like all skills, practice improves performance. Practice recognizing and categorizing normal behavior. Suspect behavior will become easy to recognize because you will not be able to place it within the Normal spectrum.

Note that the focus is on identifying predatory behavior. Since Police are the natural predators to criminals, Police are Super Predators. If you see someone acting in a predatory manner you should avoid them anyway but it is possible that they are undercover Police. Police in uniform are obvious and watching them at work can help you identify predatory behavior in a safer way.

Lastly, practice these techniques until they become second nature. Teach them to your family and friends. If you experience anything that will help me improve this book or increase the validity of the techniques, please send an email to Trikke.MI@gmail.com.

Physiology of Criminals, People, Dogs, and Cats

My research in this area indicates that people and animals can sense criminal behavior through their sense of smell but not for the reasons typically presented. There is no "crime scent" or "smell of evil". There are however, two sweat gland systems which are shared by Criminals, People, Dogs and Cats, Apocrine and Eccrine.

People Sweat

Until puberty, people have Eccrine sweat when too hot. That is for evaporative cooling. Eccrine sweat is water and salt. Grade school kids do not have to shower after recess because their Eccrine sweat doesn't decompose and smell bad and their Apocrine sweat glands are inactive.

After puberty, people have Eccrine sweat from heat and Apocrine sweat when triggered by anxiety, fear, stress and pain. Apocrine sweat contains water, salt and components that decompose when on the skin. That is what causes a bad odor. It can be considered a pheromone. Criminals generally fear being caught and crime is a very high stress job. They are most likely in a bit of Apocrine sweat at all times. Remember the old movie line "I smell a rat!"

Dogs and Cats

Dogs have very sensitive noses and can track odors left by people just walking through an area.

Some dogs receive training in following scents. They can be trained to a specific scent such as nitroglycerine or marijuana or they can be trained to follow a scent that they are given. That is typical for tracking criminals trying to escape from a crime scene.

Police Departments, TSA and other organizations have dogs that are trained detectors, most people have ordinary dogs and cats. The following paragraph explains what I believe allows the average pet to detect and alert for criminal behavior.

Dogs and cats have both Apocrine and Eccrine sweat gland systems but they are distributed differently. Their heat sweat is Eccrine and limited to their snouts and foot pads. The major sweat system is Apocrine and is at each hair follicle. This accounts for the typical smell. It acts as a territorial marker.

Now consider what the dog or cat experiences when exposed to the criminal (or fearful adult) who is expressing that Apocrine smell. I believe they consider it a territorial invasion and react accordingly. Since pre-pubertal children do not excrete Apocrine sweat, few pets are likely to treat children as threats.

Dogs will typically react to strangers in a neutral, negative or friendly manner based on their training and how they were socialized. It is not uncommon for dogs to react in a negative manner when they are normally docile or neutral. Take this as an alert for possible criminal behavior but it could be that the person is afraid of the animal and is therefore producing Apocrine sweat.

There are three principles taught here - Detect, Protect and Report

Detect

Normal Behavior

To recognize Criminal Behavior it is important to recognize normal behavior. We are pretty expert at recognizing ordinary behavior but because we have learned it through experience we usually cannot describe it accurately, we just say it is normal and leave it at that.

Going through a stop sign is illegal but most would not consider it criminal. If that driver went through a stop sign when children were trying to cross it becomes much different. The act is the same, only the exact circumstances change. We will focus on circumstances and the behaviors of predatory criminals. Please pay attention to the "small laws", especially if you have children with you, they learn faster from adult behavior than from talk.

My experience has shown that the average person speeds a little, often ignores "No Turn on Red" and a host of other annoying rules and laws. Some people are rude when driving but when out of their car where people can see them, they often become more polite.

Babies can recognize good behavior because they learn it from their care givers. They associate the smiles, laughs and delight that they observe with the comforting things they receive from those people. This by the way is the way we train cats and dogs so it shouldn't be surprising that intelligent species such as humans can adopt the same principles.

I say that we learn this through experience but to be more specific, we use all five senses to interpret the world and the people in it. It doesn't take long to identify bullies, aggressors of all sorts and parents know when their kids are lying.

However, because relatively few people are trained as Psychologists and extremely few as Behavioral Scientists, the collective experience is assigned to a category called "gut feeling, feels wrong, seems to be bad, etc."

The most important works that the author has found on Behavior Profiling are two books by Dr. Edward T. Hall. They are The Silent Language and The Hidden Dimension.

The Silent Language talks about behavior and what the body expresses through gesture, posture and other elements of behavior. Further research has amplified that data and includes micro elements such as mouth, shape, fleeting facial expressions and so forth. The field of Animation has used this information to present believable characterizations usually without recognizing its origins or acknowledging the source. I noted the focus on phonemes in teaching Animation. Phonemes are the exact placement of the lips, tongue and teeth in speech. Many animators have focused on this information but I have adopted a different approach, which grew into this book. The tongue, teeth and lips do work in a very complex way to create the voice sounds and the information has been proven by the legions of Lip Readers who have provided data on criminals, politicians and others who thought they could speak low enough to be unheard. When I began teach animation I focused on timing, not phonemes. I recalled that for hundreds if not thousands of years, puppets had been convincing speakers with only two positions, open mouth and closed mouth. No phonemes there. If the timing is right, you only need two positions. Some other teachers of animation have recognized this and continued to other elements such as posture, gait and hand, arm, leg and head movements. This gave me the clues to provide a simplified system of analyzing behavior. This way, the essential information could be learned by the average child or adult.

The Hidden Dimension had a similar impact on the research done by the author. This topic covers the way people operate in spatial terms, both by themselves and with others. Today, most people know the term personal space and know that it differs with the culture of the people. Some feel uncomfortable with physical closeness and others want to be touchy-feely. Some of the information developed through this path has made it into this book and process but most of the material herein is based on The Silent Language.

Predators

Predators take advantage of the rest of society and sometimes other predators. You cannot tell them by their looks, their clothing, what they drive or their age, sex or apparent financial condition. The simplest way for the average person to identify predators is to look at their behavior. The average person moves with a purpose. They take a direct route to their objective and waste little time getting there.

Predators, whether human or animal, seek prey and conduct risk/reward calculations to select their targets.

3 Seconds to Safety

Practice this technique until it becomes automatic. Teach your children, relatives and friends the technique. Anyone can practice it and it is proven to save lives, property and to keep people safe.

Pick someone in your environment and say out loud in simple words what they are doing. You should be instantly able to say such things as:

They are reading a book.

They are talking to someone.

They are talking to a child.

They are walking.

They are watching a performance.

They are.....

If you do not have a simple statement within 3 seconds then get away as fast as possible. I will not say you have to run, that can attract attention, but do not waste time leaving the scene.

Specific Predatory Behaviors

Predatory behaviors are divided into those which are visible at a distance and those that require a closer look. The focus of this book is mainly on distant detection. The intent is recognition of danger before the predator gets close enough to be dangerous.

You should refer to this section when preparing to report suspicious behavior to authorities. It will enhance your credibility to give specifics on why you suspect something is wrong.

This topic is so important that you need to memorize these signs and take immediate action to escape.

Attack Behaviors

People raise their arm and hand to prepare for a strike. They may pull their arm back horizontally if preparing to punch. That is the Knockout Game scenario.

Someone gives a verbal display of anger, especially if they are approaching or facing you.

Be careful of people whose hands are not visible. They may be carrying a weapon.

Tensing up is a sign of preparing to act. This behavior will be difficult to detect.

Of course, if your attempt to avoid the conflict is unsuccessful then use all means available to come out on top. You would be surprised at what the ordinary human is capable of doing when adrenalin is being pumped into the system. Gentle ladies have been known to lift cars off their husbands or children and fling criminals quite a distance.

Stalking Behavior

The criminal predator follows a general pattern which begins with selecting a type of crime, picking a territory and selecting the best times to practice their trade. Most people have experience with a regular job. Criminals are self employed for the most part but have the same job requirements that you are familiar with. The stalking part of their behavior usually includes surveillance of some sort

To avoid criminal interactions you need to watch for the typical predatory behaviors and leave the area as soon as possible. The best time to interrupt their process is in the planning stages. This is also the safest. If their process gets to the action stage it is difficult to stop and much more dangerous. So, stop them in the planning, stalking, surveillance stage for best results. Learn to recognize surveillance behavior.

Suspect Looks for a Tail

The average person doesn't check to see if anyone is following them. This is normal behavior only if someone feels threatened. Do not confuse this with someone just being cautious. If the general area is suspect most people will keep looking around (but not just behind themselves). Note: Criminals often feel threatened by the possibility of being detected so they will be constantly checking their environment for Police or a tail.

Walking and Running Behaviors

Walking at 2-3 miles per hour is average. Slower pace with stopping at interesting places is normal, especially in tourist areas. Walking at the higher rate should be straight line behavior as you would expect in someone going from one place to another with a purpose. The higher the rate of speed, the more the subject will focus on the path ahead. Anyone walking at a fast pace and looking side to side may be looking for a lost pet.

Jogging in shorts and a top is a common sight but is mostly a daytime activity. Doing that at dusk is not uncommon. Jogging at night, without lights or reflective material, is suspicious behavior. Full out running in street clothes is behavior that should raise all kinds of alarms. Any walking, running or jogging while peering into backyards or knocking on doors is highly suspect and should be reported.

Standing, Loitering or "just Hanging Around"

Most people do not stand still and quiet. Some are more agitated than others but one normal behavior connected to standing in one area is easily identifiable as waiting for someone. This includes looking in one direction where they expect to see someone, checking the time, making phone calls. This behavior often involves being near a landmark to identify the meeting place.

Hanging around in parking areas is typical of people looking to enter cars illegally. Carrying back packs or bags may seem normal but they often conceal tools used to break and enter cars and buildings.

This behavior is especially significant when the person leaving a car can be expected to be absent for more than a few minutes. Going into a Convenience Store often takes only a moment or two, too short a time for the casual thief. But if it is the parking lot of a Mall, the driver is probably gone for more than an hour which gives the criminal plenty of time to act. Similarly, the parking lot of a gym is especially attractive because the driver is almost certainly gone for an hour and, because thefts from gym lockers is quite common there is a strong possibility that ID and valuables will be in the car.

Sitting

Seldom will anyone just sit; they will watch TV or read. Ordinary sitting behavior can also be waiting for someone but that will often include some casual activity such as reading. Having a book or newspaper/magazine but not turning pages is suspect. People will normally sit in an area with some physical attraction such as a fountain, garden, statuary etc. It often involves a bench or bench substitute. Comfort is not an absolute requirement but few will pick uncomfortable spots to idle if any better spot is available.

People get on a bus or other conveyance and sit if possible. There can be a normal hesitancy about sitting next to someone but if there are open seats with no one near, beware of the person who moves close to you. Most people prefer some personal space. If there are only a few open seats then watch for other predatory behavior. Looking around is not uncommon but focusing on weak appearing individuals or sitting right by the exit when other seats are open may be a choice for quick exit after a grab and run episode.

An adult sitting on a curb or on the ground is less suspicious. It is much more difficult for most people to get up from that position. Predators will not usually reduce their ability to see around them by lowering their eye level.

Watching the Watchers

In a crowd watching some activity or show, be wary of the individual watching the audience members. Legitimate activity focuses on the object of the event. People will often glance around to see if they see someone they know or to check on their children and that is no reason for alarm. Anyone focusing on the audience is there for predatory motives (be aware that security will be displaying this behavior if they are doing their job). Look for some indication that they are identified as Security or have an official license of some kind. Security often wear uniforms and have some location where they report.

Driving Behavior

Many ordinary drivers engage in aggressive driving so that by itself does not merit attention. Extreme aggression should be reported and any identifying items such as license plate numbers and descriptions of cars and occupants should be reported. Under no circumstances should you enter into a confrontation with the other driver. If they are criminals exercising their trade they may be armed. Some have been known to bump your car to get you to stop so they can take your car or worse. Drive to the nearest Police station if possible before stopping. At least get to a public place.

Driving at night without headlights on has often meant the driver was intoxicated but with the advent of "always on headlights" they are harder to spot. Erratic driving is often intoxication but can be medical. In any case, it also needs to be reported.

In my opinion, a car with tinted windows (especially the frontal area) indicates someone who wants to hide what they are doing. If you have tinted windows and do not feel you are hiding anything then you may be the exception but an officer will take note of the tinting and may find a legal excuse (no one drives perfectly) to stop and check. Remember, one out of three traffic stops usually finds an open warrant. I also believe that having a radar detector indicates that the driver speeds more than occasionally.

Riding Behavior

Riding in this case refers to buses, trolleys or trains. It is unlikely that you will be able to note individuals riding in other cars and if they are in the car with you I would hope you have no right to suspect them of bad behavior. Airplanes are special cases and Air Marshalls are often on the plane.

People will normally sit in the first open seat unless there are other negatives such as shabby appearance of a seat mate. If someone passes up open seats to get in the rear most location it would be wise to keep alert for other behavior. The reason for getting into the back is to keep an eye on everything and perhaps to pick a target. People would find it difficult to look back over their shoulder to watch someone behind them.

Standing when seats are available is also suspect, especially if near an exit. They may be planning a grab and run maneuver.

Hyper awareness

Predators have to watch for Police, prey and for other predators. This requires constant attention to their environment. They will be constantly looking around and when they do focus, even briefly, note where their attention is directed. They will be looking for or at prey or targets for theft or people to assault.

Eye contact

Remember the words "a shifty character", the word shifty refers to eye contact. Some people do not keep eye contact well so it is not an absolute negative but should be used with other signs. It is not a sign that applies at a distance so it is not very useful for the major thrust of this book. Remember, predators look at their prey.

Personal space

Personal space is culture specific so analysis must depend on cultural norms but again, this is less useful for detecting criminals at a distance. People other than family and close friends who try to get into your personal space are often trying to get something from you that you would rather keep. Pickpockets have to be physically close to get to your wallet and may appear to be accidentally bumping into you. If you feel that someone is too close, take action immediately.

If they manage to bump you, they expect you to feel for your valuables. That shows them exactly where to go. Unless you are among family or friends, no one should be close enough to touch you. The exception is someone like a politician running for office. They should be pretty obvious but nothing is sacred and you still need to watch out. Crowds are great opportunities for thieves of all sorts. They count on distractions like good magicians.

Looking for cameras

Most businesses and many other areas have security cameras. Most people will ignore them except for the occasional glance. If someone is paying attention to cameras they may be plotting ways to avoid being seen.

Shopping Behaviors

Shoppers may spend extended periods in a store but will have some pattern such as clothing, jewelry, shoes, or other focus. Beware of someone moving amongst totally unrelated items such as going from shoes to hardware or from baby clothes to jewelry. Most people value their time enough to not just wander around looking at what is in front of them. The criminal may be looking for escape routes, random opportunities for theft and the habits of the employees.

Asking for Change

Be especially cautious if someone tries to look into the cash drawer. They have no legitimate reason to check it out. Asking for change is a common ploy to get the drawer open. Ordinary customers will often buy something such as a pack of gum to get change. People used to ask for change for a parking meter but metered parking is rarer these days and where it does exist, it often use credit cards. People hanging around idly looking at merchandise with no pattern (i.e. magazine rack, brands of similar merchandise or types of snacks) are highly suspect. They may be waiting for customers to leave so they can operate without interference. Many proprietors have a sense for this behavior but their employees may not have had training.

Dress is Inappropriate for the time, location or event

Slobs may be legitimate customers in a store but your caution level should be higher than normal. Gas stations often see people in extra casual attire but watch for behavior out of the ordinary.

Inappropriate Behavior of any kind

Any behavior that is inappropriate to the time, place and function merits serious attention. Some people with psychological problems may be showing behavioral problems without necessarily being a threat. You should still notify authorities at least for their own protection. Recently I found a man trying to unlock a car with a house key. Based on the answers to a few questions, mental confusion was identified so local Police were called and they ensured the safety of the man.

Interacting Behaviors

Friends, family and business associates often interact and make eye contact at least intermittently. Avoidance of eye contact is an indication that the other person is nervous about something. Humans have built interacting habits over the centuries and some things are characteristic of one's intentions.

A handshake begins with offering the weapon hand showing it to be empty.

Generally, the danger is less in interaction because predators are unlikely to engage in close behavior until they strike.

Writing Behaviors

Handwriting analysis is often used in detective work but the field is beyond the scope of this book. I would however advise you to be watchful of someone whose handwriting is plainly beyond the norm.

The simple analysis is that erratic handwriting is usually not associated with calm, law abiding people. At least keep an eye on those whose handwriting is clearly different.

Suspicious Behavior Summary

People are normally engaged in easily described behaviors such as walking, window shopping, talking to someone, texting, crossing the street. In short, if you cannot tell what someone is doing within a 3 second time period you should be on high alert. Criminal behavior is typically stalking and only a hunter going after prey displays this type of action. Do not become the prey!

Going back to ordinary human behavior, it is focused, task driven and time sensitive. Most people are going to perform an easily named task which may change at some point but will almost never vary in direction. Most people will never be accused of driving too slow or meandering. The exception is that teens can "just hang around" and the elderly may drive slowly but neither will typically exhibit other predatory behavior.

Some General Hints on Human Behavior

In interactions between individuals, the taller has a power advantage. That can be their natural height but it can also be artificial height. Power figures often use a platform to create that elevation. I am sure you can find many times where this tactic is used.

When two people interact as friends, they can be physically closer than if they are co-workers or strangers. Be very wary of people entering your personal space unless you have invited their attention. Many predators try to get close enough to act by devious means. If they can get inside your home, office or other non-public space they will have a huge advantage because you will often not suspect anything.

Avoid being close to anyone exhibiting aggressive or threatening behavior. The carrying of weapons other than in a hunting or target situation is by itself a threat based on the number of accidental shootings that occur.

EYES ARE THE WINDOWS TO THE CRIMINAL "SOUL"

Focus is a key term and refers to what the suspect is looking at and how intently they are maintaining that focus.

People generally look at what is attractive to them and predators look at prey.

You have been trained since birth to know where people are looking. You can tell if someone is looking at you even when they are on the opposite side of a football field.

A Soccer Goalie looks into the Striker's eyes to see where they are going to kick. The best Strikers learn how to look in one direction and kick to the other.

When I am on the Firing Range, I do not use the weapon sights, I look where I intend the bullet to go and it goes there!

Looking is a powerful tool and is perhaps better understood when it fails in use. My favorite example is the "Hallway Dance", where you meet someone and as they move to their right you move to your left and you both have to halt. This often repeats two or more times in a short time interval.

The problem is that one of you is misdirecting their eyes. One of you is looking in one direction and then moving in the other. We do this automatically and do not recognize the failure until this happens.

Another example is riding a bicycle. The rider does not "steer" their bicycle, they simply look where they want to go and the rest is automatic. If they look at a rock, they will ride right over it.

So, if someone that is not a friend or family member looks at you intently they may be evaluating you as potential prey. Be very alert if they look to see where your wallet or purse is. A favorite ploy is to ask if you can change a bill. Never make a move towards your money for anyone you don't know. If a friend asks you for change, make sure you do not flash your money.

Liars

There are many books which claim to help you tell if people are telling a lie. That takes much more study and skill and is not reliable. Even polygraphs in skilled hands can err.

Protect

Protect by avoiding criminals, criminal territories and dangerous times. This may seem obvious but I have watched people do all the wrong things without seeming to notice. Before we look at other ways to protect yourself and the ones you care about, please read the following sections and teach them to everyone. An ounce of prevention can be the cure for you.

What if I Think I am being Followed?

If you suspect someone is following you then cross the street up to three times. If someone follows once that can be coincidence. If they follow twice that is an alarm signal. Look for help or call 911. If you cross a third time and they follow you, run and when safe, call 911.

Things that we do wrong!

I watch people walk away from their car without checking the door locks. I know that the automatic locks operate in most cases because I hear the chirp. Now, if electronics never failed I could understand this but I know better. One time out of five, the lock button on my remote locks the driver door but not the sliding door. It is an old car but if an old one can fail, a brand new one can fail. Why else would we have recalls for failed parts?

I have seen a walker with ear buds on reading a book. Yes, it was daylight, it was a nice neighborhood and yes, there were other people around (mostly me). Many a robbery has occurred in such nice conditions. Criminals like to work in nice weather too.

If you cannot jog or walk without listening to music or other things that interfere with hearing at least have someone with you to monitor the area for predators.

Prairie dogs live a lot longer because of their alert system. One is always on watch for danger and when a threat appears, the alarm is sounded and everyone gets out of harm's way.

People often create what we call an attractive nuisance. That is something that is attractive to predators, thieves or anybody. This could be flashing money, wearing Designer clothes or expensive jewelry in the wrong places, leaving locks unlocked or otherwise creating a possibility of reward for a low risk. If people simply locked their locks, lockers, cars etc, we would probably reduce the crime rate by fifty percent. When I look at crime reports for the average urban area they are filled with thefts from unlocked places.

People in the United States have some common traits that abet criminal behavior and some that help identify the criminals. The most common bad thing that we do is to be predictable. We like to have schedules and stick to them. Criminals become expert at identifying patterns of behavior for the same reason that hunters observe the behavior of their prey. It makes their job easier if they can predict when and where you will appear. Of course there are things that need to be predictable such as getting to work on time but we can change our route from time to time. We definitely should not get gas at the same station at the same time. A lot of carjackings have taken place at gas stations and Mall parking lots. It is difficult to hijack a moving car but once it stops make sure all doors are locked and avoid stopping where there is no one around.

Things that we need to do right.

Protection should focus on avoiding dangerous areas, times and situations.

Dangerous areas are those known as such by Police and held to be such by common knowledge. Run down areas that receive little attention are common operating areas for criminals. They know that there will be little attention paid to what happens there. This concept is called the Broken Window Theory. Research also shows that if an area is kept neat and well maintained the people that live there care enough to watch out for and report bad elements.

There are dangerous times. One thing to consider is response time for Law Enforcement. If you have a good insurance agent you will get a discount for being close to a hydrant and they will note the distance to the Fire House. Similarly, criminals will be very familiar with the normal patrol practices and routes. Avoid being in a bad area but especially during shift change. Many departments will find it difficult to respond immediately if they are bringing officers in and sending others out. The potential for delay is not intentional but why take a chance. Avoid late night excursions, even to friendly areas. If you have to run a late errand, at least have someone with you. Follow the rules about keeping your car doors locked and avoid being blocked in. You should be able to speed away from danger at any time. No one should be allowed to approach your vehicle except a uniformed officer and even then, keep an eye open.

Dangerous situations are those in which you do not have control. Inside your home you can control most events but in public you have to depend upon the capabilities of strangers. Even the best intentions cannot prevent all bad behavior. Well lit, well attended areas with lots of surveillance cameras are better than dark areas with few people.

We want you to assist in the protection part by not presenting an easy target. Criminals do not usually seek an equal contest, they want to pick on loners and the weak or disabled. That is a common technique of predators of the animal variety and human predators copy that so at least travel in pairs if possible, four eyes can spot trouble better than two.

One of the bad human habits is predictability. Many people like routines and follow predictable behavior patterns without much thought. Predators study their prey and like it when they know what is going to happen next. Try to vary your routine, especially if you have something of value to a predator.

The other element that will keep you safer is to avoid showing tempting targets such as jewelry, designer clothing and accessories. You may enjoy them but keep them covered when you are in public spaces. You should not care how others view you unless they are friends, family or associates.

The simplest way to protect yourself is to leave the danger area before trouble starts. Some self protection advisors want you to be able to react to a situation through martial arts, weapons and such but I want you to consider that outcomes of a physical conflict are unpredictable at best and often result in harm to the innocent as well as causing expense. If the conflict becomes physical the police will be involved and either party could be charged, sometimes both. In any case you will need a lawyer and if the case goes to court you will be dependent upon the quality of the judge, jury and other participants. I believe that you should leave the physical part to the authorities. Report your suspicions using the material herein and you can return to your home to enjoy the rest of the day.

Report

First rule is that 911 is for emergencies in progress, not for suspicions. It may delay getting help if it goes to the State Police who then have to transfer the call to another jurisdiction. Use the regular phone number for the local Police (it should be in your contact list) and you should get immediate attention and since it is local it should be fast.

If you are outside the city boundaries, the Sheriff would be the logical next contact. Have their Dispatch phone number in your contacts.

When you believe you are in danger, report this to the authorities for investigation. This book gives you the language and tells you how to describe the chain of suspicion that will provide them probable cause to take action. Police will not be able to investigate because you "feel something is wrong!" Regardless of the strength of those feelings and sometimes even evidence of danger, Police must have Probable Cause before they can act.

Report suspicions in a form that will encourage investigation. Use the following method:

At approximately _____ AM or PM

On_____Street near _____(address)

Or at the intersection of _____and_____

In the City, Town, Neighborhood of _____

I witnessed the following behavior_____

The person appeared to be _____years of age, Male/Female height approximately_____

Wearing_____

The behavior that aroused my suspicions was_____

I noticed a vehicle type_____year/older/newer of _____color with a _____stripe/color with License State_____ and _____number. Photograph attached.

Case Studies

Case Study 1

The first case study involves a boat operator trying to elude a Patrol Vessel. The report came in from the Sheriff Patrol Vessel that an operator was fleeing an attempted stop. They provided a description of the boat and the operator and the direction of travel.

I was on duty at the Marine Station monitoring vessel traffic. The reported vessel was headed in the general direction of the Station but had other possible destinations.

I observed a vessel crossing the marked channel instead of entering the river. That is not uncommon because there are many destinations past the river where the station was.

What happened next was uncommon. The far side of the river has a seawall with shallow water on the other side. There was no reason to avoid the river and turn into that shallow area. But, that is exactly what the boater did. This raised a red flag.

There is a cut in the seawall upstream and it is common for boats coming from the North to enter the river through the cut. But, since it is very shallow this is not the best plan.

I got my binoculars and looked at the boat and operator. The boat did not fit the description and neither did the way the operator was dressed. While in the cut, the operator turned to look over their shoulder TO SEE IF THEY WERE BEING FOLLOWED! Only a person afraid of being followed would act like that. I sent a patrol boat to catch up to the vessel. They did and when the crew from our other patrol boat got to the scene they positively identified the operator and the boat as the one attempting to flee.

Case Study 2

I was in a village market in the Philippines. It was early evening. I observed a man loitering near a lamp pole. Loitering is a first sign of predatory behavior. The background is that natives in that area and time had often came into town and had killed people. This man was wearing a trench coat which was another bad sign since the temperature was above 90 degrees Fahrenheit. The third sign of trouble was when the coat gapped a bit; a Thompson Sub Machinegun could be seen. This would seem to be time for quick action and I began looking for some protective barriers. I was relieved when the Police car arrived and they joined in a conversation. The Police car was Jeep with a .50 caliber machinegun which will give you an idea of the potential for trouble. The man was an "undercover" Policeman. This is a good time to point out that Policemen are Super Predators who exhibit all the threatening behaviors that I am warning you to avoid. Of course, avoiding Policemen may be unnecessary but it does no harm. If they are in uniform it will be pretty obvious that they present minimal threat. If they start taking action you will want to be out of the line of fire.

Case Study 3

The following report is from one who attended a seminar and learned how to detect possible criminal behavior. They, and I, believe that this was a significant event.

Location: Springfield, Illinois, July 2014, early evening. Elderly man, wife and daughter.

I pulled into the city parking lot and observed a man about 30 years old loitering and he looked at me. We proceeded to check into our Hotel. We decided to have dinner at a restaurant across the street. The man that I had observed earlier trailed behind us into the restaurant and took a seat at the bar. He was shortly joined by another man. We finished our meal and left the restaurant walking on the sidewalk. The second man seemed to follow us then he crossed the street heading for our hotel. The first man also came out and joined the second in front of our hotel. We quickly entered a hotel on the side of the street we were on because there were no other people outside. We asked for a Security escort to get into our hotel and they complied. The Security Guard recognized the two men as street people, not hotel residents.

This set of events almost certainly identifies the behavior of the two men as Predators and the proper reaction of the gentleman in seeking protection prevented a bad outcome. It caused no harm.

My views on some hot topics and some advice

Drug crimes

Drug use is a solo crime. The perpetrator and the victim are the same person. Addiction was, is and will be a problem for rehabilitation, not incarceration. Making a medical-social-psychological problem into a criminal behavior creates millionaires out of drug dealers who would have a hard time working at a fast food franchise. Just as with our experiment in prohibiting alcohol, the profit potential for trading in illicit products generates attendant problems ranging from corruption to the thefts that abusers use to support their habit. I am not proposing legalization of drug use, de-criminalization is the goal. This would cut the prison population to leave room for dangerous felons that prey on innocent people. Those felons are being let out due to crowding increasing the threat to law abiding citizens. The economic advantages to de-criminalization are multitude ranging from the ability to tax the traffic to the savings received from the lower costs of rehabilitation over incarceration. Of course the reduction in crime might cause a temporary unemployment problem in law enforcement but I am sure we can find other tasks that would benefit from more resources.

Decriminalization of Drugs

A commentator asked if someone you loved was doing heroin would you call a Policeman or a Doctor. The answer was obvious. Drug abuse is a medical problem as are most abuse patterns such as smoking. There are others hurt by the behavior either through injury, theft to support habits, operating vehicles while under the influence and so forth but the crime is a self inflicted one.

The jails and prisons are filled with people who cannot benefit from the punishment and the cost of incarceration far outweighs what it would cost to provide rehabilitation. Rehabilitation is not always successful but even the failures can continue at lesser cost than the present system.

The Violent Society

I have noted a high level of anxiety in my family and friends which is attributable to the almost daily reports of gun violence in the media. The situation is not good but it is better than you might think. Violence is the current hot topic so reporting that problem gets more air time than many other events. The amount of time that broadcasters can devote to stories is called the News Hole. There is almost always more news that there is room so only the hottest topics get aired. The facts are that mass murders, typically a father killing his children, his wife and then committing suicide, has decreased in frequency over the last few decades to approximately 20 per year. Again, this is not good but it is better than in the past.

What is often portrayed as random violence is seldom random. The victim's address book is often the best place to start looking. Siblings fight because others don't care enough to bother arguing. They just walk away. Similarly, few strangers will hate you enough to attack, especially with guns, knives and other lethal devices.

When a neighborhood gets shot up, it often involves drugs, sex or other criminal activities. If the neighbors had reported those activities they could have been quashed before coming to a head. If you ignore bad behavior of any kind it is not likely to go away on its own. I am not saying that innocent people don't get hurt, only that people need to keep their neighborhood safer by keeping the Police informed of crimes, criminals and any suspicious behavior.

Gun Violence

The United States is famous world-wide for the fascination with the old west and the famous gun fighters. The John Wayne and gangster type movies kept the ball rolling. The United States is also filled with hunters. There is nothing wrong with hunting whether for sport or food but it means that guns are common and many people consider them as part of their attire. We also have a large group of people who fear home invasion and believe that they need to protect their home with weapons. I know of very few criminals who just want to invade homes. They go looking for money, valuables, drugs, etc. If you make people aware that there are attractive targets inside then it is prudent to keep protective measures at hand. Unfortunately, many people who keep guns for protection simply provide a convenient weapon for the intruder to use. Most people do not spend time at the range perfecting their response to threats and their marksmanship.

Based on recent news of gun violence including armed robberies, people shooting up homes and threatening behavior with guns, I have tried to identify the type of person that commits gun crimes.

For the most part, I do not believe that these people have a concealed weapons permits. They certainly do not display attention to other rules. They are likely to be involved in other criminal activities rather than having a normal job. It seems that they have anger management problems because most normal people would not escalate arguments to gun level.

I would say that armed robbers focus on banks, armored cars, jewelry and illegal businesses likely to have large amounts of cash on hand. If none of these are part of your daily routine I think it would be safe to say that you can be less concerned with that threat.

The threat to neighbors where domestic violence occurs is that if bullets fly, they could go anywhere. Any domestic dispute can escalate to violence. Report disturbances and take cover. Anyone subject to any type of abuse should recognize the potential for death or injury to themselves and others so they have to take the lead in getting medical and legal assistance.

One common cause for neighborhood violence is drug deals that go bad or people not paying their bills to the dealers. The dealer cannot take the customer to court so they take corrective measures on their own and the customers are usually no better at abiding by the law than the sales people. This is the problem that could disappear with the de-criminalization of drugs. Let us presume that if you, your family and your associates are not using drugs then the threat would have to come from neighbors that do. If you report any suspicious behavior in your neighborhood the likelihood of this problem will be greatly reduced.

Open Carry

Since most of the laws regarding carrying a weapon specifically talk about Concealed Weapons, it has caused many people to try open carry where not outlawed. (Be mindful that if you get into a car, the weapon is then concealed and you will need the CCW permit).

I would never carry openly when out of uniform. I do not want the criminals in the area to know where the gun is or that anyone is prepared to take action. Why give up the element of surprise?

Carrying a weapon openly gives the criminals full knowledge of the location and time to study how to take it from the owner. The owner will not always be able to retain possession against a determined criminal who can call in assistance if they desire.

Fire Arms Instructors have called open carry tactical suicide.

A Policeman on duty realizes that the visibility of the weapon is part of his armory. It is a low level use of force which prevents more problems from escalating than you might imagine.

Gangs and Gang violence

Most of the information in this book talks about a lone predator or a few working together. Gangs have different behavior, more like packs. There is a leader and a few followers. It would be well to avoid them but especially if they have an audience that they want to impress. They will often dress in similar fashion for group identification but also to make describing individual members more difficult.

If you see three or more people wearing similar clothing and moving as a unit they are either a parade or a gang. It does little harm to avoid them.

Carjacking

Please note that old rusty cars are seldom the target of carjacking. If someone wants to steal a car and risk the penalty, they are likely to go for the better models. There are also cars which are easier to steal than most and some offer greater rewards for parts on the chop shop scene. If you have one of the more attractive models you need to be proactive in your defense. Never let yourself get boxed in. Carjacking is usually a stopped car event so you want to be able to speed away from danger. Do not act in a predictable fashion. Do not go to the same places at the same times. Avoid stopping in lonely or dark areas. Be especially alert when exiting and approaching your vehicle. Try to see into the vehicle if approaching to see if anyone is in there. The back seat is a common place to hide. Try to avoid traveling alone.

Mental Illness

When mental hospitals were closed, the people needing medical assistance were forced into more public arenas and in cases where medication is useful it is more difficult or impossible to monitor the administration of the medicine. Meanwhile, the emphasis on civil liberties makes it more difficult to bring people to treatment unless they volunteer for it. Combine this with the public perception of mental illness and you have a guarantee that people needing help will often not get it until they threaten or injure others.

For people with mental illness but not otherwise dangerous the probability that their behavior will hold clues to their potential for harm allows us to apply the Behavior Profiling principles to get out of harm's way.

Needless to say, people with dangerous mental challenges (the type to commit murder or mayhem) are seldom going to seek treatment on their own and they often express paranoia which can make benign actions seem threatening.

The Anti Movement

Recently we have seen an increase in individuals and groups who preach and practice Anti-Government and/or Anti-Society principles. They object to things that they claim are against the Constitution. Some claim to be "Sovereign Citizens" and that they are therefore immune to prosecution under the laws and regulations that govern our society. Law Enforcement is a bigger target for this group than ordinary citizens but because of their beliefs, there is a high potential for fights of all kinds including arson. If you encounter this behavior it would be wise to leave the area immediately.

Petty Crimes

We live in a society where casual disobedience seems to be the norm. People driving will coast through a stop sign quite often and not think anything about it. Traffic rules such as not crossing a double yellow line are violated so often that it is most surprising when the rule is not violated. Traffic Engineers use that visible sign when the danger is high that crossing that area is most likely to cause an accident. Part of the problem may be that the Engineers are overly cautious and put them where they are not really needed. It is likely that the people ignoring the speed limits are also ignoring most other safety regulations. The only time most people obey these kinds of rules is when a Police vehicle is near and visible. In any case Law Enforcement people can take advantage of these habits because they create a scenario where the vehicle can be stopped for investigation. The driver has created a "Probable Cause" situation. Experienced Law Enforcement people can confirm that simple traffic stops for infractions such as No Signal, Light not operating, Plate or Tab expired, etc can find real criminals. About one in three traffic stops finds someone in the vehicle with an open warrant for their arrest. It could be something simple such as unpaid traffic tickets or non-payment of child support but it is still an offense.

Summary

I BELIEVE IN THESE PRINCIPLES

This book is meant to tell you someone could be a danger. The techniques are easy to learn and reliable. Take a step of faith and follow these principles. I am absolutely sure of their validity.

I do not normally wear body armor. I feel safer detecting threats by observation than by depending on mechanical devices.

Recommendations

One very important tool is the Acme Thunderer Police whistle. It is loud and attracts a lot of attention. Attention is the last thing a predator wants.

Check with your local jurisdiction to see if carrying Pepper Spray is legal and if so, in what form and how much can be carried. (If Pepper Spray is illegal then remember that Pepper is a condiment. You can always carry a packet of ground pepper for your pizza.) It works the same because it is the same. Note, even Police Pepper Spray doesn't work on everyone.

You may not need a cane for walking but it is a style accessory and it can be used to hit someone (or something).

Keep a dummy wallet (or purse) and a dummy key ring with car and house keys. Put a few one dollar bills in it and add those dummy credit cards and dummy ID cards that fill your mail box. Pick up an old wallet from the resale store so it looks right.

With a dummy purse, you can get physical if you keep a large can of baked beans in it. Swing hard and fast if you need to.

If someone wants your car or house keys and you haven't been able to escape, consider throwing the keys as far as you can as an option. You need to consider how the predator will react but the net result is that they will not have your vehicle as transportation or access to your house for burglary, at least without searching.

If you are walking, jogging or running, keep all your senses on high alert. If you must use ear buds, stick to the treadmill where you will be safer. There are many hazards to being outside with your hearing impaired. Remember, having someone with you is safer than being alone.

Advice on Locks and Lockers

Combination locks need to be spun after closing to ensure that the slots are not lined up. If you don't spin the dial, the lock will open with a sharp blow.

Key locks can be quickly opened with a vibrating pick. Combination locks are better. Do not use chains; they can be quickly cut by even small bolt cutters that can be hidden under a coat. Cables are much harder to cut and usually resist bolt cutters, even big ones.

Pick storage locations that are in the open. Thieves will take advantage of natural cover.

Anyone hanging around is highly suspect. Normal behavior is coming, doing something or going. There are exceptions but keep an eye on those people.

Guard Dogs

The proper title should be Alert Dogs. Dogs should not be used to guard things. Anyone willing to commit burglary, robbery or home invasion will not likely be stopped by any animal. They will either buy it off with a large piece of meat or simply dispose of it. No dog is equal to an armed and determined criminal. They will do a great job of alerting you to the presence of intruders long before they can enter your home, office, store or whatever. Once they have alerted you to the intruder, you have the chance to notify police. Reward them for their expertise; do not put them in harm's way.

If the preceding information raises your level of alertness and makes you more sensitive to the behavior of others then it has accomplished its goal.

Lastly, Lock things up

I present Seminars on Criminal Behavior Profiling and to prepare for those I check the crime statistics for the area for a few weeks prior to the seminar. It became obvious after a short while, that most communities could cut their crime rate in half by simply getting people to lock their doors, cars and lockers where they store valuables. Ask any Police department and they will tell you that if people took care to avoid thefts they would have time to concentrate on serious crimes and the people stealing things left available would have to seek legitimate work. Most are unwilling to train for higher level crimes that need tools and techniques.

Authors Expertise

BA in Sociology, Oakland University

10 years teaching Geographic Profiling

10 years of teaching Animation

Electronic Warfare Specialist, U.S. Navy

Marine Safety Officer

Seminars are available, contact me at Trikke.MI@gmail.com.

If you have comments or wish to ask a question, also contact me at Trikke.MI@gmail.com. I will attempt to reply as soon as possible.

Attendees have used the Behavior Profiling techniques to prevent many crimes. The report in Case Study 3 was submitted by one who attended a recent seminar.

References

Crime Score – Criminal Behavior Profiling for seniors written by William J. Riley

Available from Amazon Kindle, Google Play Books and Apple I Books

The Hidden Dimension – How people interact with spatial elements by Dr, Edward T. Hall

The Hidden Language – Communicating through Body Language by Dr. Edward T. Hall

Crime Reports – local newspapers often provide a summary of local crimes. There is a national organization that you can subscribe to at www:crimemapping.org. Many communities provide data to them and it is often in almost real time.

If you are suspicious about some potential harm to National Security you can notify the local FBI office, Customs and Border Patrol or Homeland Security

Many communities have Alert systems that can send you a text message when circumstances require extra care and attention to suspicious behavior.

Many communities have Neighborhood Watch Programs. These are effective if they are active.

Operation Predator is an Alert Service provided by the Department of Homeland Security as ICE Alert. Go to www:ice.gov/predator/predatorapp

Partners include Internet Crimes Against Children Task Force ICAC, Interpol and the National Center for Missing and Exploited Children.

If you have some information regarding Border Security, National Security, Customs or Interstate Crimes then the FBI is a good choice to go to.

Many local communities are providing text message alerts and feedback systems for crime reporting and special problems. If you do not have this then you could propose it for your area.